Published in the UK by
POWERFRESH Limited
3 Gray Street
Northampton
NN1 3QQ

Telephone 01604 30996
Facsimile   01604 21013

GW01218455

Cover and interior layout by Powerfresh

ISBN 1 874125 686

Printed in the UK by Avalon Print Northampton
Powerfresh August 1997

" WHAT TIME DO THEY TEE OFF ? "

"ON THE OTHER HAND DENNIS, IT WAS A GOOD GAME FOR THE NEUTRALS."

"DON'T TELL ME YOU'VE PUT YOUR BACK OUT DOING THE MEXICAN WAVE AGAIN?"

" I SAW YOU KISSING THAT NUMBER TEN ON THE TELLY!"

" WHAT ARE YOU DOING WITH THAT APPLE, ADAM?.. "

"WE'LL NOT BE A MINUTE. ERIC'S JUST PUTTING HIS FACE ON..."

"WELL I THINK IT'S A RIDICULOUS IDEA, MAKING THE GOALKEEPER CAPTAIN."

"ONE OF SOCCERS LEGENDARY HARD MEN."

" WELL JUST WHERE THE HELL ARE YOUR PROPER GOALKEEPING GLOVES? ..."

" YOU CAN BORROW SOME OF MY TAPE FOR YOUR SHIN PADS IF YOU LIKE..."

" JUST WHEN IS THIS TEAM GOING TO SIGN A GOALKEEPER?".

" IT WAS A SHOULDER CHARGE REF..."

" I THINK YOU MAY HAVE DESIGNED THE ULTIMATE FOOTBALL BOOT, LEWIS..."

"IT'S SOME NEW F.I.F.A RULING."

"SO YOU'RE CONFIDENT YOU HAVE THE BACKING OF THE BOARD?..."

" THEN AGAIN FRANK, THE PITCH IS THE SAME FOR BOTH TEAMS."

" EXACTLY HOW OLD ARE THESE STRIPS BOSS? "

IT'S ABOUT TIME WE GOT THIS DIRECTORS BOX MODERNISED.

"IT'S ALRIGHT BOSS, THE T.V. CAMERAS HAVE GONE."

" BRING ME THE GROUNDSMAN!.. "

" WE'RE GOING TO HAVE TO THINK ON A LARGER SCALE FOR THE PREMIERSHIP, MR CHAIRMAN... "

"IT'S TAKING HIM A WHILE TO ADJUST FROM THE PITCH TO THE BOARDROOM."

" WHERE'S THAT TRANSFER MONEY? "

"APPARENTLY THE COMMENTATOR IS A BIT SHORT SIGHTED"...

"YOU MUST UNDERSTAND DOCTOR, WE WANT HIM BACK IN TRAINING AS SOON AS POSSIBLE.."

" OUR LACK OF SUBSTITUTES IS BEGINNING TO TELL "..

" I HEAR YOU'RE QUITE INJURY PRONE."

"JUST HOW BADLY INJURED IS THIS PLAYER?"

"GORDON!, GORDON, SHOULDN'T WE TRY THE SPRAY FIRST?"..

"THERES DEFINATLEY A LANGUAGE BARRIER WITH THAT NEW FOREIGN SIGNING".

"I'M AFRAID THAT'S ALL YOU GET OF HIM FOR TWO AND A HALF MILLION".

" JUST WHAT KIND OF A BOOT DEAL HAVE YOU GOT, ERIC ? "

" ALRIGHT, I'M CONVINCED. WE'LL SIGN HIM... "

"ARE YOU NERVOUS AT ALL IN YOUR FIRST CUP FINAL SON?"

" IS THIS THE FIRST TIME YOU'VE ORGANISED A DEFENSIVE WALL CYRIL?".

" I KNOW IT'S YOUR BENIFIT SEASON STAN, BUT... "

"WELL AT LEAST STEVE DID HIS BEST TO STOP THAT FREE KICK."

" WATCH OUT FOR THE QUICK FREE KICK".

"ADMIT IT PETER, YOU'RE GETTING PAST IT."

" HE'S SUSPENDED FOR THREE GAMES "

" CHANGE OF TACTICS LADS, WE'RE GOING TO START MAKING MORE USE OF
THE LONG BALL .."

" WHAT DO YOU MEAN? , SHAKING HANDS TOO HARD ! " ...

" FOR TIME WASTING ..."

" WILL YOU STOP PROTESTING THE REFEREE ROY! WE'VE ONLY LOST THE TOSS.."

"EXACTLY HOW MUCH TIME ARE YOU ADDING ON REF?"

" WHAT DO YOU MEAN?, YOU'VE LEFT YOUR FLAG AT HOME!!"

"AT LEAST THE REF GOT A GOOD VIEW OF THE INCIDENT"

"THE REFEREE MUST HAVE MADE A GOOD DECISION."..

"AND I DON'T WANT TO HEAR YOU CALLING ME SHORT SIGHTED AGAIN, HARRISON!..."

"YES I KNOW IT'S TRADITION TO SWAP SHIRTS AT THE END OF THE GAME, BUT I REALLY DON'T SEE THE POINT..."

" I TOLD YOU THAT REFEREE WAS BIASED "...

"YOU'RE JUST SUPPOSED TO CHECK ONE BOOT AT A TIME.."

CRINKLED 'N' WRINKLED

DRIVEN CRAZY

TRUE LOVE

IT'S A BOY

IT'S A GIRL

NOW WE ARE 40

FUNNY SIDE OF 30s

FUNNY SIDE OF 40 HIM

FUNNY SIDE OF 40 HER

FUNNY SIDE OF 50 HIM

FUNNY SIDE OF 50 HER

FUNNY SIDE OF 60'S

FUNNY SIDE OF SEX

FLYING FUNNIES

SEX IS...

FOOTNOTES

SPLAT

PEEPING TOM

MIDLIFE CRISIS

WE'RE GETTING MARRIED

THE ART OF SLOBOLOGY

THE DEFINITIVE GUIDE TO VASECTOMY

KEEP FIT WITH YOUR CAT

MARITAL BLISS AND OTHER OXYMORONS

THE OFFICE FROM HELL

PMT CRAZED

SEXY CROTCHWORD PUZZLES

STONED AGE MAN

OUT TO LUNCH

HORNY MAN'S ADULT DOODLE BOOK

HORNY GIRL'S ADULT DOODLE BOOK

IF BABIES COULD TALK

CAT CRAZY

MAD TO TRAVEL BY AIR...

MAD TO PLAY GOLF...

MAD TO HAVE A BABY...

MAD TO GET MARRIED...

MAD TO HAVE A PONY

MAD TO HAVE A CAT

MAD TO HAVE A COMPUTER

YOU DON'T HAVE TO BE MAD TO BE 40 HIM

YOU DON'T HAVE TO BE MAD TO BE 40 HER

YOU DON'T HAVE TO BE MAD TO BE 50 HIM

YOU DON'T HAVE TO BE MAD TO BE 50 HER

MAD ON FOOTBALL

For more information on these or other titles please write to :
Powerfresh Ltd. 3 Gray Street, Northampton, NN1 3QQ, ENGLAND.
Telephone 01604 30996 Fax 01604 21013